LET'S TALK ABOUT
Abortion

Carly Kol ✶ Emulsify

This book is dedicated to anyone who has ever had or will ever have an abortion(s).

This edition first published in 2025 by

Crocodile Books
An imprint of Interlink Publishing Group, Inc.
46 Crosby Street
Northampton, Massachusetts 01060
www.interlinkbooks.com

Text copyright © Carly Kol , 2021, 2025
Illustrations copyright © Emulsify, 2021, 2025
Designed by Emulsify

All rights reserved. No part of this publication may be reproduced, stored in a retrieval system or transmitted, in any form or by any means, without the prior written permission of the publisher.

Library of Congress Cataloging-in-Publication Data available.
ISBN 978-1-62371-620-2

10 9 8 7 6 5 4 3 2 1

Printed and bound in China

LET'S TALK ABOUT
Abortion

Carly Kol ✳ Emulsify

Crocodile Books, USA
An imprint of Interlink Publishing Group, Inc.
www.interlinkbooks.com

A Note from the Creators

When we released the first iteration of this book under the title *What's an Abortion, Anyway?* in 2021, we were existing in a desperate political and legal landscape for abortion seekers and havers. At the time, there were very few resources for kids about abortion care that were medically accurate and gender-inclusive.

As we release the second iteration of this resource in 2025, abortion access has only been further eroded for millions of people around the United States. Despite this, few new resources have been created to support conversations between adults and kids about what abortion care is and why people have abortions.

With updated text, images, and content, this book is intended to support adults in introducing the concept of abortion to kids in a purely factual way, devoid of political framing and without imposing morality. While we deeply believe in abortion liberation—access to care for everyone, everywhere, at any time, and for any reason—this book is meant to provide a foundation for you and the little ones in your life to explore abortion in your unique community's context.

In order to engage with this book, the reader must have a basic understanding of how pregnancy happens. There are many fantastic books that help explain the fundamentals of reproduction and pregnancy; we list them on page 30.

The images in this book are based on the likeness of real individuals who have had abortions thanks to *We Testify*, an abortion storytelling nonprofit that invited their network to submit self-portraits for our book. Additionally, the doctor pictured on page 15 is the likeness of Dr. Jamila Perritt, a long-time abortion provider in Washington, DC.

There are different words and ways to explain abortion to kids. We recognize that language is forever changing; the words in this book were intentionally chosen as most appropriate at the time of publication.

Throughout this book, you will notice that we refer to abortion havers and seekers as "pregnant people." It was important to us that this book honors everyone who has abortions and challenges the mainstream social assumption that only cisgender women have abortions.

While every child develops at a different pace, this book has been vetted by a panel of early-childhood educators, ensuring its language is age-appropriate and its content is accessible to readers ages 6-12.

As the political, social, and legal landscape around abortion forever shifts, we hope that our book provides grounding, clarity, and comfort to you and the children in your life. As we say in the book, abortion has always existed, and it always will. We owe it to our littles ones to never waver on our commitment to the dignity and autonomy of all abortion havers and seekers—the ones we love and the ones we will never know.

When a person gets pregnant, many different things can happen.

Some people are pregnant for many months and have a baby. That's what happened with you!

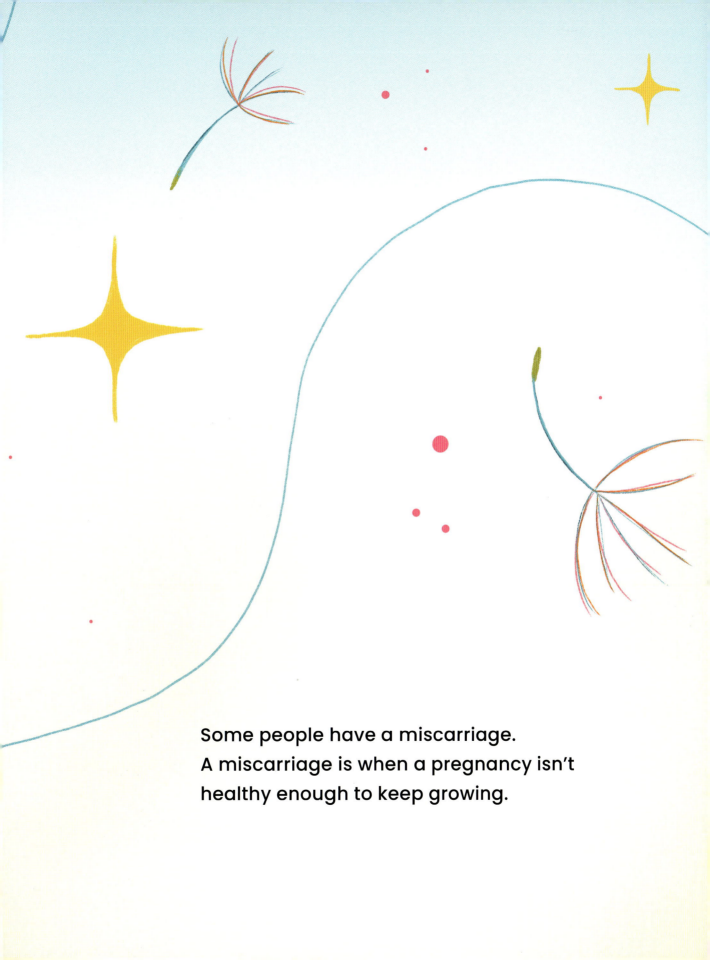

Some people have a miscarriage.
A miscarriage is when a pregnancy isn't healthy enough to keep growing.

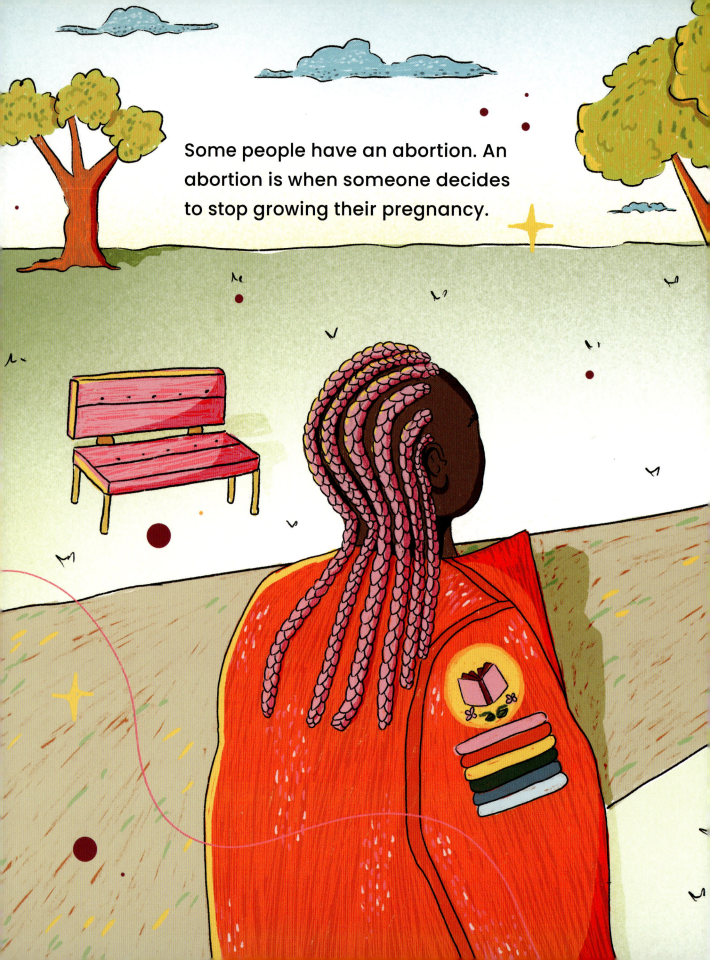

People have abortions for different reasons.

Some people have an abortion because they like their family exactly as it is.

Some people have an abortion because they can't take care of a new baby right now.

Some people have an abortion because their doctor says pregnancy could make them sick.

No matter the reason, everyone should be able to decide what's best for themselves, their bodies, and their families. Only you know what your body needs!

There are different ways to have an abortion.

Some people see a doctor who does a special procedure to remove the pregnancy from inside their body.

Other people take medicine to stop the pregnancy from growing bigger.

Sometimes people can decide how they want to have an abortion, and sometimes they can't. It might depend on where they live or how big their pregnancy has grown.

No matter how people have an abortion, everyone deserves to do it when and where they want.

People can have different feelings before, during, and after their abortion.

Some people want to talk about it, and some people don't.

Some people feel happy or calm.
Some people feel sad or lonely.

Many people feel all of these things at the same time. There is no right or wrong way to feel!

No matter how people feel, everyone deserves to be treated with love and respect. We can never know what it's like to be someone else!

People have abortions every day, all around the world.

Most people know and love someone who has had an abortion.

No matter what, people have always had abortions, and they always will.

Resources

We have always viewed this book as a missing piece in the larger resource network that kids need and deserve in order to fully conceptualize the spectrum of pregnancy outcomes. Here are some additional recommended resources on reproduction and pregnancy outcomes.

Books about the fundamentals of reproduction

- *What Makes a Baby* by Corey Silverberg
- *Making A Baby: An Inclusive Guide to How Every Family Begins* by Rachel Greener and illustrated by Clare Owen

Books about miscarriage

- *Dear Star Baby* by Malcolm Newsome
- *Always Sisters: A Story of Loss and Love* by Saira Mir and illustrated by Shahrzad Maydani

Books about adoption

- *Eyes that Weave the World's Wonders* by Joanna Ho and Liz Kleinrock and illustrated by Dung Ho
- *A Kids Book About Foster Adoption* by Jamie Murnane

Books about grief

- *Goodbye: A First Conversation About Grief* by Megan Madison and Jessica Ralli and illustrated by Isabel Roxas
- *Grief is an Elephant* by Tamara Ellis Smith and illustrated by Nancy Whitesides

Discussion Questions

The following questions are intended to support conversations about abortion between young readers and trusted adults. Abortion can be a hard topic for adults to talk about with each other—let alone with kids!

We invite you to stay open and curious, and we hope these questions can lead to deeper, more nuanced conversations that ground abortion in the context of the reader's own life and community.

- Have you heard the word "abortion" before? If so, what did you know about it?
- Why do you think some people have abortions?
- How do you think some people feel about their abortions?
- Do you know anyone who has had an abortion?
- Sometimes, adults can have big feelings about abortion. Some adults think abortion should be allowed for all pregnant people, and others don't think abortions should be allowed at all. What do you think?
- What additional questions do you have about abortion?

Facts about Abortion

Due to the politicized nature of abortion, it can even be hard for adults to discern what is true about abortion and what is social stigma. Below are some simple facts that you can share with kids to help ground them in universal truths about abortion.

- People of all genders, races, and religions have abortions.
- People have abortions at all different stages of pregnancy.
- Abortion is a form of health care.
- People all over the world have abortions.
- Some people have more than one abortion during their lifetime.
- Abortion is a safe medical procedure when done with a trained provider.

Acknowledgments

This book started out as a community-funded project on Kickstarter in 2021, and we are grateful to the 546 backers who helped bring the first iteration of this book to libraries, schools, abortion clinics, and more than 5,000 young readers across the world.

We send our love and appreciation to our friends, family, and community members who read the many draft iterations of this book and provided beautiful edits and insights since its inception in 2017.

Lastly, we want to thank all of the abortion providers, abortion funds, practical support organizations, abortion companions, and legal advocates who work tirelessly every day to support abortion havers and seekers.

Emulsify (they/them) is a queer parent and full-spectrum doula. They create art to imagine new worlds. Emulsify lives in Brooklyn with their family and spends a lot of time creating while snuggling their pups. Through their work, they have made incredible friendships, learned from brilliant peers, and found their home.

Carly Kol (she/her) is a white, queer, Jewish full-spectrum doula from New York. She has always believed that young people deserve honesty and compassion when it comes to information about their sexual health and bodies. Carly has supported over 3,000 individuals during their procedural abortions and medication abortions. She currently lives in Los Angeles, California with her partner and their pit bull, Mickey.